YOUR M&S Cookbook

Christine France

MARKS &
SPENCER

Marks and Spencer p.l.c.
PO Box 3339
Chester CH99 9QS

s h o p o n l i n e
www.marksandspencer.com

ISBN: 978-1-84805-501-8

Printed in China

Written by Christine France
Photography by Clive Streeter
Home Economy by Angela Drake and Teresa Goldfinch
Designed by Talking Design
Edited by Fiona Biggs

With special thanks to Sarah Loxton, Laura Fernandez and Gayle McDermott.

Notes for the Reader
All products included in the M&S Ingredients range are subject to availability.

This book uses both metric and imperial measurements. Follow the same units of measurement throughout; do not mix metric and imperial. All spoon measurements are level: teaspoons are assumed to be 5 ml, and tablespoons are assumed to be 15 ml. Unless otherwise stated, milk is assumed to be full fat and eggs and individual vegetables are medium.

The times given are an approximate guide only. Preparation times differ according to the techniques used by different people and the cooking times may also vary from those given. Optional ingredients, variations or serving suggestions have not been included in the calculations.

Recipes using raw or very lightly cooked eggs should be avoided by infants, the elderly, pregnant women, convalescents and anyone suffering from an illness. Pregnant and breastfeeding women are advised to avoid eating peanuts and peanut products. Sufferers from nut allergies should be aware that some of the ready-made ingredients used in the recipes in this book may contain nuts. Always check the packaging before use.

CONTENTS

It's no surprise that M&S have a fine reputation for good food, and many of us have been relying on their food section for many years to provide us with time-saving, good-quality, ready meals and inspirational fresh ingredients.

However, these days, you'll find that there's so much more – take a look on the shelves in the M&S food department and you'll discover a huge new range of really useful storecupboard ingredients, too.

There's everything from the most everyday items like herbs and spices, flour and sugar, right through to more unusual, gourmet ingredients such as dried porcini mushrooms, avocado oil and coconut flakes. In fact, there's just about everything you'll need to produce all kinds of dishes at home, from cup cakes to casseroles, all in one shop. It's all designed to make your food shopping quicker and easier – in fact, much less stressful and far more enjoyable!

What's more, M&S have taken great care in selecting the very best produce available for their range of essential ingredients, so there's no confusing choice of different types, shapes and sizes of products to compare – that's already been done for you, so you're faced with, quite simply, the best of each item. Everything in this range of ingredients has been carefully and ethically sourced.

If you're looking for inspiration for hassle-free everyday meals, just choose one of the ready-blended spice mixes, carefully prepared to make speedy, perfectly spiced curries and casseroles based on exciting flavours from around the world. They will make even the most basic ingredients into an exotic feast.

Add a selection of grains and pulses to your storecupboard and you'll never be short of the basis for a main meal – be adventurous and try bulgar wheat, quinoa or lentils for a quick and healthy, high-fibre main dish or accompaniment, or make a statement with some red rice for a sophisticated dinner party dish.

For those occasions when time is tight and you need to prepare a celebration treat for someone special, M&S have everything you need. Look out for time-saving cake or cookie mixes, ready-made frostings and decorations, or speedy cheats to help you whip up special desserts in minutes, such as ready-made, all-butter pastry cases, or prettily piped meringue baskets. For those on a restricted diet there's even M&S Gluten Free Plain Flour, and since our M&S Baking Powder is also gluten free there's no need for anyone to miss out on home-made cakes and bakes.

A one-stop M&S food shop offers all the ingredients you need to stock up your storecupboard, together with fresh and healthy produce too, making it easy for you to produce balanced, speedy weekday meals for the family, food for impressive dinner parties and tempting treats on baking days.

MARKS &
SPENCER
WHOLE
NUTMEG
flavour with...
freshly grate into
cakes, puddings,
milk sauces,
and mash potato
MARKS &
SPENCER
CARAWAY
SEEDS
flavour with...
to add a sweet aniseed
spiciness to stews,
breads, vegetables
and biscuits

These days, we have so many demands on our time that cooking a meal often slips way down on the list of jobs to be done.

With today's busy lifestyles it's hardly surprising that we find ourselves looking for shortcuts in the kitchen. But fast food doesn't have to mean junk food. Whether you're just feeding yourself and want to eat in a healthy way, or you're providing daily meals for a hungry family, the key is buying the right ingredients.

Every chef worth his or her salt will tell you that sourcing good-quality ingredients is the basis of good cooking. If you can count on the basics, it makes life so much easier – you're halfway there and the rest will follow more smoothly.

A well-stocked storecupboard packed with useful basics and flavourings will ensure that you always have the core ingredients for a meal – then all you need is a quick top-up shop for the fresh additions as and when you need them.

At the end of a hard day, none of us wants to feel resentful about cooking a meal, or indeed guilty about not eating healthily, so anything that helps with the decision about what to cook is a help. Even the most inexperienced cook can follow some simple, well-written pack instructions. So be adventurous and have a go! Don't be afraid to take short cuts, especially with products you know you can trust.

Even if you've never cooked with yeast before and find the prospect a little daunting, a pack of ready-yeasted bread dough mix will help you make a perfect pizza that works every time – far better than any takeaway, and you won't have to worry about buying and mixing the yeast. A pack of risotto mix is a failsafe way to whisk up a really tasty one-pot meal that doesn't involve lots of preparation and fuss.

Canned foods are often underestimated, although they can be incredibly convenient. Canned pulses such as chickpeas or red kidney beans can really save time in the kitchen as there's no need for soaking and long cooking – just drain and heat. Jars of ready-chopped garlic, chopped herbs or roasted peppers also deserve a place in any good storecupboard.

When it comes to seasoning and adding flavour, many of us tend to err on the cautious side; after all, once you've added too much chilli or salt it's not easy to correct. But with a well-balanced, carefully proportioned spice mix, the guesswork is largely taken out for you. Then, when you become more confident, you'll be encouraged to start making your own blends from scratch with whole spices.

Few of us want to spend all day, every day, cooking but once you familiarize yourself with good-quality ingredients, cooking will become less of a chore – you may even find you enjoy it!

Time-Saving Tips for Clever Cooks

If you're looking for time-saving tips in the kitchen, the storecupboard is a good place to start. Whether you're short of time after work for everyday meals, or simply want to avoid spending hours in the kitchen when you have guests for dinner, M&S have endless ways to help you cut a few corners – with no compromise on quality and flavour.

If you prefer using real stock instead of stock cubes but haven't the time to have a stockpot boiling for hours, keep a pouch of M&S Stock handy for adding a rich depth of flavour to soups and casseroles. Or a jar of M&S Stock Concentrate is an easy way to add just a spoonful of flavour to sauces and gravies.

Keep a selection of speedy seasonings for adding an instant boost to ordinary meals. Pep up plain fish or meat with a conveniently packaged spice mill mix to grind just the right amount of rich flavour without hours of marinating. These mixes are versatile too – coarsely ground M&S Smoked Chilli & Garlic Mill makes a simple grilled steak sensational, or can season a quick savoury butter to melt over a baked potato or corn on the cob.

Spice pastes and dry mixes offer the opportunity to prepare ethnic dishes with quite complex flavours without the need for grinding and blending spices. Authentic dishes made from scratch may have as many as a dozen spices, all separately ground and toasted for a genuine flavour, but with an M&S spice paste all the preparation is done for you, so you can add the fresh meat, fish or vegetables and take all the credit for a spicy, home-cooked jalfrezi curry or tagine.

Stir-fries and noodle dishes are popular for easy meals, and they can be on the table in minutes, especially if you have ready-made sauces to stir in. A slosh of M&S Hoi Sin Sauce or Oyster Sauce with quick wok noodles or egg noodles and a sprinkling of chilli flakes can turn simple vegetables into an Oriental feast. For Mediterranean inspiration, keep jars of sundried tomatoes, passata, peppers, roasted garlic and chopped basil to add instant sunshine to a bowl of pasta even in the depths of winter.

When time is really tight and you need to conjure up a meal in a matter of minutes, one of the best storecupboard standbys is M&S Microwaveable Rice. In only $1^1/2$ minutes, the long grain, basmati or wholegrain rice is ready to serve, either as a simple accompaniment, or as the base for a complete main dish – stir in sundried tomatoes, a drained jar of roasted peppers, diced ham, canned tuna or whatever takes your fancy to make a really tasty, instant pilaf.

MARKS &
SPENCER

SMOKED CHILLI
& GARLIC MILL

flavour with...
grind over meats
and oily fish for a
fleshy aromatic
fragrant marinade

MARKS &
SPENCER

DRIED
PORCINI
MUSHROOMS

cook with...
risottos, pasta and
omelettes to add
an earthy aroma...
just steep in hot
water first

A Cheat's Guide to Survival

Cooking really is a relaxing pleasure at times, and it can be satisfying to spend an afternoon pottering in the kitchen, chopping and stirring, making wonderful food for friends and family. But few of us have time to cook from scratch every day, and it's hard to shop to cover every eventuality. A well-stocked storecupboard should have a few secret weapons to help you cope with pretty much any culinary emergency, any day of the week.

Routine family meals can be a nightmare to cater for and if you're cooking meals to feed a hungry family every day, especially if you're juggling with work commitments too, it's hard to be inspired for seemingly endless weeknight cooking. So it's helpful to stock up on a few items that will help you to get by without too much stress.

A jar of M&S Korma or Balti Paste, for instance, will transform a few odds and ends into a really tasty curry that all the family will love – and it's a great way to use up leftovers of cooked meat and vegetables to make another meal. Pasta sauces and canned tomatoes are invaluable, too, for quick and healthy meals.

It's not easy to keep fresh herbs in the refrigerator for regular use and it can be wasteful to buy large fresh bunches or pots, but they make all the difference so it's worth keeping jars of ready-to-use 'wet' herbs, such as M&S Coriander, Parsley or French Thyme, in the refrigerator to add a fresh herb flavour.

Unexpected guests for dinner? If extra guests arrive and there's not enough food to go round, make a casserole go further by adding a can of M&S Chickpeas or Butterbeans. Soak M&S Bulgar Wheat for an easy, no-cook accompaniment. Ready-made pastry cases are a godsend when you have to rustle up a quick quiche or some pretty fruit tartlets, and meringue nests can transform seasonal berries into a no-fuss, sophisticated dinner party dessert.

When you need a squeeze of lemon juice on your pancakes or grilled fish, but all you have in the refrigerator is a tired lemon, a bottle of M&S Lemon or Lime Juice will save the day.

If you like to make home-baked treats for the family, or for friends dropping in for coffee, turn to a good pack of cake mix. M&S Victoria Sponge Cake Mix is a reliable family favourite, and can be converted into a lavish strawberry gateau for an impromptu summer celebration.

How about fancy cup cakes for a children's birthday party? Finish muffins with ready-to-roll icing, then let the children have fun writing their names on top with colourful M&S Writing Icing, while you put your feet up!

Even if you're able to shop regularly for fresh foods, a well-stocked storecupboard is a huge help in preparing meals of all kinds. With the fast pace of life we're all faced with these days, a little organization and forward thinking helps to make shopping and planning for meals an easier task

Although storecupboard items can be invaluable, if you over-buy and hoard too many items, you'll find it hard to use them while they're still at their best. Your storecupboard should be a back-up for the fresh items that form the main part of meals, with a few useful supplies for emergencies.

Everyone's needs are different, but this checklist may help you to decide what you need to fit in with your style of cooking, tastes and lifestyle.

Essential Staples:
Flours – plain, self raising, wholemeal, bread flour, cornflour
Sugars – caster, granulated, icing, demerara, muscovado
Dried pasta – selection of small shapes and long pasta
Rice – basmati or long grain, risotto, wholegrain, pudding
Dried beans and pulses – lentils, haricot beans
Sea salt and black peppercorns

Useful Basics and Standbys:
Dried herbs – parsley, thyme, bay leaves
Spices – cinnamon, mixed spice, coriander
Oils – sunflower, olive, avocado, sesame
Grains – bulgar, couscous, polenta, quinoa
Egg noodles – medium or fine
Dried fruits – sultanas, raisins, mixed fruit, cranberries, dates, apricots
Nuts and seeds – almonds, hazelnuts, pine nuts, sunflower, pumpkin
Canned beans and pulses – chickpeas, butterbeans

Wine vinegars, balsamic and flavoured vinegars
Canned tomatoes, whole or chopped
Passata
Tomato purée
Worcester sauce
Oriental sauces – Thai fish sauce, oyster sauce, soy sauce
Pouches of stock, or concentrated stock paste
Leaf gelatine
Cooking chocolate and cocoa
Golden syrup, maple syrup and honey
Canned fish – tuna, salmon
Canned fruits

Shortcuts and Secret Weapons:
Microwaveable rice
Jars of chopped garlic, shallots, 'wet' herbs, chillies
Spice pastes – tagine, korma, balti
Spice dry mixes – tandoori, methi chicken, rogan josh
Dried mushrooms – mixed or porcini
Sundried tomatoes, dried or in oil
Pasta sauces, pesto
Risotto mixes
Roasted peppers in oil, artichoke hearts in oil
Balsamic glaze
Ready mixes – bread dough, batter, dumpling, stuffing mixes
Dried breadcrumbs
Cake, muffin and cookie mixes
Ready-made icings and frostings
Vanilla sugar
Cinnamon sugar
Meringue nests or mini meringues
Ready-made pastry cases

Quick & Easy

AVOCADO BULGAR LUNCH SALAD

For a healthy summer lunch or lunchbox, this easy salad is packed with protein, antioxidants and vitamins. Both avocado and avocado oil are rich in antioxidant vitamin E, and also contain a high proportion of monounsaturated (or 'good') fat.

1. Place the bulgar wheat in a large, heatproof bowl and pour over the boiling water. Cover and leave to stand for 30 minutes.

2. Meanwhile, cut the avocado in half, remove the stone and scoop out the flesh with a large spoon. Slice crossways into chunky slices and place in a bowl with the tomatoes, chickpeas and feta cheese.

3. To make the dressing, place the lemon juice, avocado oil, parsley and garlic salt, and black pepper in a screw-topped jar and shake well to mix thoroughly.

4. Drain the bulgar wheat and stir in the dressing, then toss with the avocado mixture and adjust the seasoning to taste.

5. If not serving immediately, the salad can be covered with clingfilm and kept in the refrigerator for several hours.

Serves 4–6

200 g/7 oz M&S Organic Bulgar Wheat
1.1 litres/1⅞ pints boiling water
1 ripe avocado
200 g/7 oz cherry tomatoes, halved
410-g/14½-oz can M&S Organic Chickpeas, drained
200 g/7 oz feta cheese, crumbled
2½ tbsp M&S Organic Sicilian Lemon Juice
5 tbsp M&S Organic Avocado Oil
1½ tsp M&S Parsley and Garlic Salt Mill, coarsely ground
M&S Black Peppercorns, freshly ground

Cook's Tip
To speed up the cooking of the bulgar wheat if time is tight, place it in a saucepan with the water and bring to the boil, then simmer gently for 10–15 minutes until the water is absorbed and the bulgar wheat is tender. Stir in the dressing and add the remaining ingredients.

ASIAN-STYLE PRAWN NOODLE BOWL

Oriental noodle dishes are always a favourite, but sometimes there's lots of slicing and chopping to be done. In this hassle-free, low-fat recipe, everything is ready to simply tip in and then cook in one pot! Even better, it is ready to serve in less than 5 minutes.

1. Heat the stock with the hoi sin sauce in a large saucepan or wok and bring to the boil. Add the noodles, stir to break up and leave over a low heat for 4 minutes.

2. Stir in the pak choi and bring to the boil. Stir in the bamboo shoots and prawns and simmer for 2 minutes.

3. Divide the noodles between 4 serving bowls and pour over the liquid. Serve immediately, with soy sauce for sprinkling to taste.

Serves 4
2 x 500-g/1 lb 2-oz pouches
   M&S Fish or Chicken Stock
1 tbsp M&S Hoi Sin Sauce
245-g/8¾-oz pack M&S Medium
   Egg Noodles
200 g/7 oz baby pak choi, halved
150-g/5½-oz pouch M&S
   Bamboo Shoots, drained
300 g/10½ oz large peeled,
   cooked king prawns
M&S Ketjap Manis Soy Sauce,
   to serve

Cook's Tip
You can vary the flavourings in this noodle bowl depending on your taste. M&S have a great selection of oriental choices — try adding a sprinkling of chilli flakes, some crumbled M&S Kaffir Lime Leaves or a piece of M&S Star Anise.

EASY-PEASY PIZZA

Making your own pizza is easier than you might think – this simple recipe cuts out most of the effort by using a convenient pack of bread mix for the base, kneaded using an electric mixer or food processor. So your preparation takes only minutes, with none of the usual kneading by hand.

1. Cover the sundried tomatoes in hot water and soak for 20 minutes. Brush a large baking sheet with oil.

2. Stir 1 teaspoon of the oregano into the bread mix and add lukewarm water according to the pack instructions. Leave to rest for 5 minutes, then knead with an electric mixer or food processor for 5 minutes, or knead by hand for 10–15 minutes.

3. Roll out the dough on a lightly floured worktop to a 33-cm/ 13-inch round and place on the baking sheet. Cover loosely with oiled clingfilm and leave in a warm place for 30–40 minutes, until doubled in size.

4. Preheat the oven to 220°C/425°F/Gas Mark 7. Spread the passata over the dough. Roughly chop the tomatoes and scatter over the dough with the mozzarella. Mix the remaining oregano with the remaining oil and drizzle over the pizza. Sprinkle with sea salt and black pepper.

5. Bake in the preheated oven for 15–20 minutes, until risen and golden brown. Serve hot.

Serves 4

65-g/2¼-oz jar M&S Italian Sundried Tomatoes
3 tbsp extra virgin olive oil
2 tsp M&S Dried Oregano
375-g/13-oz pack M&S White or Wholemeal Bread Mix
6 tbsp passata
125-g/4½-oz ball buffalo mozzarella, chopped
M&S Sea Salt and Black Peppercorns, freshly ground

Cook's Tip
Vary the topping by adding extra ingredients from the storecupboard, such as a jar of M&S Roasted Red and Yellow Peppers, or Grilled Artichoke Hearts, drained, with a handful of black olives. For a thin-crust pizza, divide the dough into two and make two thin pizzas instead of the basic deep crust.

TUNA LINGUINI

Pasta can always be relied on for quick, healthy meals, but it's easy to run out of serving ideas. Roast garlic and Italian herbs give this dish an instant, rich Mediterranean flavour, with crumbled sundried chillies for heat. You choose the amount of chilli — use one for mildly spiced, two for a hotter kick.

1. Bring a large saucepan of lightly salted water to the boil. Add the linguini and cook for 11 minutes, or according to pack directions, until al dente. Drain well.

2. Place the emptied pan over a medium heat, add the oil, stir in the garlic, herbs and chilli peppers and remove from the heat. Add the pasta and toss thoroughly to coat evenly. Roughly flake the tuna and stir into the pasta with the olives.

3. Adjust the seasoning with sea salt and black pepper, then divide the pasta between 4 bowls and serve, sprinkled with freshly grated Parmesan cheese.

Serves 4
450 g/1 lb dried linguini
1 tbsp olive oil
1 tsp M&S Roasted Garlic, drained
3 tbsp M&S Italian Blend Herbs
1–2 M&S Sundried Chilli Peppers, crumbled
418-g/14¾-oz can tuna steak in brine, drained
100 g/3½ oz stoned black olives, quartered
M&S Sea Salt and Black Peppercorns, freshly ground
freshly grated Parmesan cheese, to serve

Cook's Tip
If you prefer, the canned tuna can be replaced with fresh tuna steak. You will need four tuna steaks, about 115 g/4 oz each, brushed with olive oil. Cook the steaks under a hot grill or on a griddle for 6–8 minutes, turning once. Flake and stir into the pasta.

QUINOA PILAF WITH PANCETTA

A great alternative to rice, quinoa is richer in potassium and iron than other grains, and it's also high in B vitamins, especially B6, niacin and thiamine, all very important for a healthy metabolism. So this easy-to-make, tasty main meal dish just happens to be good for you, too.

1. Place the mushrooms in a small heatproof bowl and pour over boiling water to just cover. Leave to soak for about 20 minutes.

2. Rinse the quinoa in cold water then place in a large saucepan with 1 litre/1¾ pints lightly salted water and bring to the boil. Cover and simmer for 15 minutes, then drain well.

3. Meanwhile, heat the oil in a large frying pan and quickly fry the onion and pancetta, stirring frequently, for 3–4 minutes, until starting to brown. Add the courgettes and cook for a further minute, stirring.

4. Drain the mushrooms and stir into the frying pan, then remove from the heat. Drain the quinoa well, then stir into the other ingredients. Adjust the seasoning to taste with sea salt and black pepper.

5. Sprinkle the pumpkin seeds over the pilaf and serve hot, with yogurt for spooning over. A green salad would make a good accompaniment.

Serves 4
17-g/½-oz pack M&S Dried
  Mixed Mushrooms
200 g/7 oz M&S Organic Quinoa
1 tbsp olive oil
1 onion, thinly sliced
300 g/10½ oz pancetta cubes
2 courgettes, coarsely grated
40 g/1½ oz M&S Organic
  Pumpkin Seeds, toasted
M&S Sea Salt and Black
  Peppercorns, freshly ground
150-g/5½-oz pot natural yogurt,
  to serve

Cook's Tip
To make the recipe even simpler, replace the onion with a jar of M&S Shallots, drained before use. For a special meal, add a drizzle of M&S Porcini Oil with Black Truffle just before serving. For a vegetarian alternative to the pancetta, add some grilled halloumi cheese.

LIGHT & EASY MACKEREL BRUSCHETTAS

For a quick lunchtime filler, these rustic bruschettas will fit the bill perfectly, and you can feel very virtuous as they're packed with healthy ingredients. Smoked mackerel fillets, conveniently ready-to-eat and bone-free, are rich in protein and omega-3 fatty acids, the type of fats that may prevent heart disease as part of a healthy diet.

1. Preheat the grill to hot.

2. Roughly flake the mackerel fillets with a fork, then stir into the ricotta cheese with the dill and lime juice. Season to taste with sea salt and black pepper.

3. Brush both sides of the bread slices with oil and toast under the grill for 1–2 minutes until golden brown, turning once.

4. Spoon the mackerel mixture onto the toasts, sprinkle with sunflower seeds and serve with a few rocket leaves, if using.

Serves 4

175 g/6 oz smoked mackerel fillets, skinned
250-g/9-oz pack ricotta cheese
1 tsp M&S Dried Dill Tops
1½ tbsp M&S Organic Lime Juice
2 tbsp olive oil
8 chunky slices from a ciabatta loaf
2 tbsp M&S Organic Sunflower Seeds, lightly toasted
M&S Sea Salt and Black Peppercorns, freshly ground
handful of rocket leaves, to serve (optional)

Cook's Tip
This mackerel and ricotta cheese mixture can also be used as a filling for M&S Pastry Spoons as instant party nibbles to serve with drinks — a sprinkle of smoked paprika looks good on top. Or simply spoon into M&S Savoury Pastry Cases for a quick snack.

CHUNKY CHORIZO WINTER SOUP

This hearty, economical main-meal soup needs only a few minutes of your time, as it can be left to simmer over a low heat while you get on with other things. The balanced soup mix of peas, lentils and pearl barley gives a protein-packed boost on a chilly winter's day.

1. Place the soup mix in a bowl and soak in plenty of cold water for 8–12 hours or overnight. Rinse in cold water and drain.

2. Heat the oil in a large saucepan and fry the leeks and squash for 2–3 minutes, stirring often, without browning. Add the stock and bring to the boil, then add the drained soup mix, bay leaves and chorizo.

3. Return the soup to the boil, then reduce the heat, cover with a lid and simmer gently for 30 minutes. Adjust the seasoning to taste with sea salt and black pepper.

4. Serve the soup in bowls sprinkled with chopped parsley, if using, and with crusty bread to soak up the delicious juices.

Serves 4

500-g/1 lb 2-oz M&S Organic Soup & Casserole Mix
2 tbsp M&S Pure Sunflower Oil
1 leek, trimmed and sliced
1 small butternut squash, peeled, deseeded and cut into 1-cm/½-inch dice
1 x 500-g/1 lb 2-oz pouch M&S Beef or Chicken Stock
2 x M&S Dried Bay Leaves
115 g/4 oz chorizo in one piece, cut into 1-cm/½-inch dice
M&S Sea Salt and Black Peppercorns, freshly ground
chopped flat-leaf parsley (optional) and crusty bread, to serve

Cook's Tip
If you don't have time to soak the beans overnight, simmer them in a saucepan of water for 30 minutes instead, then drain before adding to the recipe as above. If the soup is not eaten straight away it tends to thicken as the pulses absorb more liquid, so if necessary add 200–300 ml/7–10 fl oz extra stock or water to thin it to the right consistency.

THAI-STYLE CRAB & SWEETCORN PANCAKES

Based on a mix of Thai flavours, these little drop pancakes are very simple to make from storecupboard ingredients. A batter mix makes a handy base for many sweet or savoury dishes, from traditional pancakes or Yorkshire puddings, to seasonal fruit clafouti puddings or crisp, batter-coated fish.

1. Tip the batter mix into a bowl, then add the coconut milk, egg white and Thai green curry paste, beating with a wooden spoon or hand whisk until evenly mixed.

2. Reserve a few spring onion slices for garnish and add the rest to the batter with the sweetcorn.

3. Heat a large, heavy frying pan or griddle until very hot and brush with oil. Drop tablespoonfuls of the batter into the pan and cook for about 2 minutes on each side, turning once, until golden brown. You will need to cook the pancakes in 3–4 batches. Remove and keep warm while cooking the remainder.

4. To serve, spoon the crabmeat onto the pancakes, top with a little oyster sauce and scatter the reserved spring onions over the top. Serve hot.

Serves 4

128-g/4½-oz pack M&S Batter Mix
200 ml/7 fl oz M&S Coconut Milk
1 egg white
100g/3½ oz M&S Thai Green Curry Paste
5 spring onions, thinly sliced
325-g/11½-oz can sweetcorn, drained
M&S Pure Sunflower Oil, for shallow frying
2 x 170-g/5⅞-oz cans white crabmeat in brine, drained
3 tbsp M&S Oyster Sauce, to serve

Cook's Tip
This recipe uses half a 200-g/7-oz jar of M&S Thai Green Curry Paste and half a 400-ml/14-fl oz can of M&S Coconut Milk. You can use the rest for a Thai chicken or prawn curry (recipe on the curry paste jar label). For a lighter batter, replace the coconut milk with water.

QUICK PORK & APRICOT MEATLOAF

If you're looking for something economical to tempt the family for a weekday meal, look no further. Not only is this unusual meatloaf full of flavour, but most of the work is already done for you — we've used a delicious apricot and herb stuffing as a base, so all you need to do is mix and bake!

1. Preheat the oven to 200°C/400°F/Gas Mark 6. Grease and base-line a 1-litre/1¾-pint loaf tin.

2. Tip the stuffing mix into a bowl and pour over the boiling water. Stir to mix evenly, then leave to stand for 5 minutes.

3. Place the mince in a large bowl and break up with a fork. Add the soaked stuffing mix and sea salt and black pepper to taste, stirring well to mix thoroughly.

4. Spoon the mixture into the prepared tin and press down evenly. Cover the tin with oiled foil and bake in the preheated oven for 35–40 minutes, until the meatloaf is firm and shrinking away from the sides of the tin.

5. While the meatloaf is cooking, tip the tomatoes into a saucepan and add the smoked paprika with sweet pepper and thyme. Stir until boiling, then simmer for 2–3 minutes to reduce the juices slightly. Stir in any juices from the meatloaf.

6. To serve, run a knife around the edges of the meatloaf, then turn out onto a serving plate. Serve in slices, with the tomato sauce spooned over and fresh rocket on the side. The meatloaf is equally good served hot or cold.

Serves 4

M&S Pure Sunflower Oil, for greasing
1 pack M&S Apricot & Herb Stuffing Mix
300 ml/10 fl oz boiling water
500 g/1 lb 2 oz lean pork mince
400-g/14-oz tin M&S Organic Peeled Plum Tomatoes
1 tsp M&S Smoked Paprika with Sweet Red Pepper & Thyme Mill
M&S Sea Salt and Black Peppercorns, freshly ground
fresh rocket, to serve

Cook's Tip
To make the meatloaf a little more special, line the loaf tin with overlapping thin slices of bacon before filling with the mixture. Other types of mince can also be used for this recipe — turkey mince makes a particularly good alternative to pork, as it's also low in fat.

Weekend Cooking

MOROCCAN LAMB STEAKS

An easy recipe to choose when you're entertaining friends, as timing is not too critical here. Based on the classic Moroccan tagine, this dish is cooked gently with a richly spiced sauce. We've paired it with cous cous stirred with fennel seeds for a change, which gives a delicious aniseed-like flavour.

1. Heat the oil in a large flameproof casserole over a moderately high heat, add the lamb steaks and fry for 2–3 minutes to brown, turning once. Add the onion and cook for a further 2 minutes until golden.

2. Stir in the tagine paste, apricots, tomatoes, olives, and some sea salt and black pepper and bring to the boil. Reduce the heat to low, cover tightly and simmer gently for about 1 hour.

3. Meanwhile, heat the oil and fry the fennel seeds for a few seconds, stirring. Remove from the heat, add 300 ml/10 fl oz water, then stir in the cous cous. Cover and leave to stand for 10 minutes or until the water is absorbed. Stir in the flaked almonds and serve with the lamb.

Serves 4
2 tbsp olive oil
4 lean lamb leg steaks
1 large onion, sliced
200-g/7-oz jar M&S Tagine Paste
175 g/6 oz M&S Dried Organic Apricots
400-g/14-oz tin M&S Organic Chopped Tomatoes
100 g/3½ oz stoned green olives
M&S Sea Salt and Black Peppercorns, freshly ground

To Serve
1 tbsp olive oil
2 tsp M&S Fennel Seeds
200 g/7 oz M&S Organic Cous Cous
4 tbsp M&S Organic Flaked Almonds, toasted

Cook's Tip
The lamb can be cooked the day before you need it, then cooled, covered and refrigerated overnight. You'll find that the flavours will develop more on reheating and become even richer than before. When you're ready to serve, simply reheat gently and prepare the cous cous.

SALMON & GRUYÈRE FISH CAKES

Fish cakes are well worth making and they're easier than you may think. These combine flaked salmon with delicately flavoured Gruyère cheese for added richness. Oatmeal gives a crunchy, high-fibre crust, and they're best when cooked with very little oil, which is good for the diet, too!

1. Peel the potatoes and cut into chunks. Bring a large saucepan of lightly salted water to the boil, add the potatoes and cook for 15–20 minutes, or until tender. Drain well and mash roughly.

2. Flake the salmon into small chunks and stir into the potato with the onions, cheese and black pepper to taste. Divide the mixture into 8 patty shapes. (For smaller fish cakes, shape into twelve.)

3. Mix the oatmeal with the sea salt with rosemary and lemon in a shallow bowl. Dip the fish cakes in the oat mixture, pressing lightly and evenly.

4. Brush a large, heavy-based frying pan with oil and heat until very hot. Add the fish cakes and cook over a medium heat for 8 minutes, turning once, until golden brown. Drain on absorbent kitchen paper. Alternatively, brush the fish cakes lightly with oil and cook under a hot grill, turning once, until golden.

5. Serve the fish cakes hot, on a bed of baby salad leaves, topped with a spoonful of mayonnaise and a sprinkling of capers.

Serves 4
1 kg/2 lb 4 oz floury potatoes, such as Maris Piper
2 x 213-g/7½-oz can wild Canadian red salmon, drained well
5 spring onions, trimmed and finely chopped
100 g/3½ oz Gruyère cheese, coarsely grated
125 g/4½ oz M&S Organic Coarse Oatmeal
1 tbsp M&S Sea Salt with Rosemary & Lemon
M&S Pure Sunflower Oil, for brushing
M&S Sea Salt and Black Peppercorns, freshly ground

To Serve
1 bag baby salad leaves
4 tbsp mayonnaise
3 tbsp M&S Salted Capers, rinsed and drained

Cook's Tip
It's important to drain the potatoes very thoroughly, or the fish cakes may be too wet and soft. The fish cakes can be made up to 24 hours in advance, covered with foil or clingfilm and stored in the refrigerator until you're ready to cook

SMOKED CHILLI & GARLIC CHICKEN WITH PORCINI MUSHROOMS

The simplest dishes are often the best when you're entertaining, as they leave you free to enjoy time with your guests. This is a good example, as the chicken can be prepared in advance, covered and kept in the refrigerator, all ready to pop into a hot oven. It looks impressive too!

1. Preheat the oven to 200°C/400°F/Gas Mark 6.

2. Lay out the chicken breasts on a board, smooth side down, and, holding a sharp knife parallel to the board, cut a long slit through the side of each, opening out to make a pocket.

3. Sprinkle the inside of each pocket generously with coarsely ground smoked chilli and garlic spice. Divide the soaked porcini mushrooms between the chicken breasts, tucking firmly into the pockets. Wrap the chicken over to enclose.

4. Wrap the chicken breasts with the pancetta to hold the mushrooms in place, then arrange in a shallow ovenproof dish and sprinkle generously with more coarsely ground smoked chilli and garlic spice. Tuck the sprigs of tomatoes around the chicken and pour over the wine.

5. Bake in the preheated oven for about 20 minutes, until lightly browned and the chicken juices run clear, not pink, when the meat is pierced. Allow the chicken to stand for 5 minutes before serving.

6. To serve, lift out the tomatoes and the chicken breasts and cut the chicken breasts in half diagonally, arranging the 2 pieces overlapping on serving plates. Spoon over the juices and serve hot, with baby new potatoes and a fresh green salad.

Serves 4

4 skinless chicken breast fillets
M&S Smoked Chilli and Garlic Spice Mill
20-g/¾-oz pack M&S Dried Porcini Mushrooms, soaked in hot water and drained
8 strips thinly sliced smoked pancetta
4 sprigs cherry vine tomatoes
100 ml/3½ fl oz dry white wine
baby new potatoes and a fresh green salad, to serve

Cook's Tip
If you wish, save the soaking liquid from the porcini mushrooms and add to the cooking juices. If there is too much liquid, simmer it for a minute or two to reduce slightly.

BALSAMIC-GLAZED PORK WITH BUTTERBEAN & PEPPER MASH

A really easy storecupboard 'cheat' recipe that looks impressive enough for a dinner party. The rich, dark balsamic glaze not only gives a really lovely, intense flavour to the meat, but a quick swirl of it on a stark white plate makes the dish look stunningly professional!

1. Preheat a ridged griddle pan to very hot.

2. Firstly brush the pork steaks with the balsamic glaze and sprinkle with sea salt and black pepper. Leave this to soak in for a minute then lightly drizzle the steaks with the sunflower oil and add to the pan. Reduce the heat to moderately hot and cook the pork for 10–12 minutes, turning once, until golden brown and no longer pink inside.

3. Remove the pork from the pan, cover with foil and leave to rest for 2–3 minutes. Meanwhile, tip the butterbeans into a saucepan and heat gently until almost boiling, then drain, return to the pan and mash lightly with a fork. Add the garlic and peppers, season with sea salt and black pepper and stir until evenly heated. Stir in any juices from the pork.

4. Divide the bean mash between 4 serving plates, top each with a pork steak and finish with a swirl of balsamic glaze. Garnish with a sprig of flat-leaf parsley, if using.

Serves 4

4 lean pork loin steaks
1 tbsp M&S Balsamic Glaze, plus extra to garnish
M&S Pure Sunflower Oil, for greasing
410-g /14½-oz tin M&S Organic Butterbeans
1 tsp M&S Roasted Garlic
285-g/10¼-oz jar Roasted Red & Yellow Peppers in Oil, drained and cut into chunks
M&S Sea Salt and Black Peppercorns, freshly ground
flat-leaf parsley, to garnish (optional)

Cook's Tip

It's important to get the pan really hot before cooking the pork, to achieve a well-browned surface with clear griddle lines. This recipe also works well with other lean meats such as chicken breast or, for a vegetarian alternative, grilled halloumi slices are good too.

SPICED BEEF & ORANGE KOFTAS WITH SUNSHINE SALSA

These spicy minced beef kebabs are great for informal entertaining, and they're economical, too. The fresh, colourful orange and tomato salsa is packed with vitamin C and antioxidants lutein and lycopene.

1. Soak twelve bamboo skewers in water for at least 30 minutes, to prevent them burning when grilled.

2. For the salsa, finely grate the zest from the orange and reserve, then cut away all the peel and white pith with a sharp knife. Carefully remove the segments, chop roughly and mix with the tomatoes, 2 teaspoons of coriander, 1 tablespoon of olive oil and sea salt and black pepper to taste.

3. Place the minced beef in a large bowl and add the orange zest, the onion, the harissa paste, the remaining coriander, the pine nuts and the egg. Season well with sea salt and black pepper and mix well. Divide the mixture into twelve and use your hand to mould each piece around a bamboo skewer, in an oval shape.

4. Preheat the grill to hot. Place the koftas on a lightly oiled baking sheet and brush with oil. Grill for 10–12 minutes, turning occasionally, until golden brown. Use a palette knife to help you to turn the skewers, to prevent them breaking up.

5. Serve the koftas hot with the salsa and pitta breads.

Serves 6

1 large orange
2 tomatoes, diced
2 tbsp M&S Coriander
2 tbsp olive oil
700 g/1 lb 9 oz lean minced beef
1 onion, finely chopped
1 x 90-g/3¼-oz jar M&S Harissa Paste
55 g/2 oz M&S Organic Pine Nut Kernels
1 large egg, beaten
M&S Sea Salt and Black Peppercorns, freshly ground
pitta breads, or cooked rice, to serve

Cook's Tip
All the preparation for this dish can be done earlier in the day, so there are no last-minute panics. Shape the koftas on the skewers and make the salsa, cover with clingfilm and chill in the refrigerator until you're ready to cook

BAKED RED RISOTTO WITH WALNUTS & PORCINI MUSHROOMS

Making risotto usually involves constant stirring while the rice cooks, but in this case, it cooks itself in the oven, leaving you to make the rest of the meal or spend time with your guests. The result is a rich, amber-coloured risotto that makes a satisfying, healthy vegetarian main course.

1. Preheat the oven to 200°C/400°F/Gas Mark 6. Pour boiling water over the porcini mushrooms to just cover and leave to soak for about 20 minutes.

2. Melt the butter and oil in a wide, flameproof casserole and fry the onion for 2–3 minutes until soft but not browned. Add the rice and stir until all the grains are coated in oil. Stir in the wine and cook for 2 minutes until almost all the wine has been absorbed.

3. Stir in the hot stock, the porcini mushrooms with their soaking liquid, and the thyme, and season with sea salt and black pepper. Cover with a tight-fitting lid and bake in the preheated oven for 15–20 minutes until the rice is just tender and most of the liquid is absorbed.

4. Stir in the walnuts, sprinkle with the Parmesan cheese and serve hot.

Serves 4

20-g/¾-oz pack M&S Dried Porcini Mushrooms
25 g/1 oz butter
1 tbsp olive oil
1 red onion, chopped
300 g/10½ oz M&S Italian Risotto Rice
200 ml/7 fl oz red wine
3 tsp M&S Vegetable Stock Concentrate, dissolved in 500 ml/18 fl oz boiling water
2 tsp M&S French Thyme
100 g pack M&S Organic Walnut Pieces
55 g/2 oz Parmesan cheese, grated
M&S Sea Salt and Black Peppercorns, freshly ground

Cook's Tip
For a lighter-flavoured, creamier risotto, use white wine instead of red and replace the red onions with white onions. Sliced, fresh closed-cup mushrooms can replace the porcini, and 2–3 tablespoons of cream can be stirred in at the end of cooking.

SWEET POTATO & CASHEW NUT TATIN

An unusual, colourful vegetarian dish that can also double as a side dish to serve with grilled or roast meats. Polenta makes a surprising partner for Indian spices, but it works well, providing a mild base to offset the more powerful, rich curry flavours.

1. Preheat the oven to 200°C/400°F/Gas Mark 6. Lightly brush the inside of a 23-cm/9-inch cake tin with oil. Bring a saucepan of lightly salted water to the boil, add the sweet potato and cook for 8 minutes.

2. Meanwhile, heat the remaining oil in a heavy-based saucepan, add the onion and cook for 2 minutes, stirring. Add the spices from sachet 1 of the Bombay potato spices pack and fry for a few seconds. Add the sugar and vinegar to the pan and stir over a medium heat for about 1 minute. Remove from the heat and stir in the drained sweet potato and cashew nuts, stirring to coat evenly. Sprinkle over the contents of sachet 2 of the Bombay potato spices pack, stirring to mix, then spoon into the prepared tin, pressing down lightly.

3. Bring 800 ml/1⅜ pints of water to the boil in a large saucepan and add the polenta in a steady stream, stirring constantly. Cook for about 1 minute, stirring until it thickens, then remove from the heat and season to taste with sea salt and black pepper. Spread it evenly over the vegetables in the tin with a palette knife. Bake in the preheated oven for 25–30 minutes, until the polenta is firm and beginning to shrink from the sides of the tin. Leave to stand for 2 minutes then run the point of a knife around the edge and turn out onto a warmed serving plate.

4. Serve the tatin hot, as a main course with a fresh tomato salad, or as a side dish with meats.

Serves 4–6
3 tbsp M&S Pure Sunflower Oil
600 g/1 lb 5 oz sweet potato, cut into 15-mm/⅝-inch dice
1 small red onion, cut into 15-mm/⅝-inch dice
1 pack M&S Bombay Potato Spices
1 tbsp M&S Dark Muscovado Sugar
1 tbsp M&S Malt Vinegar
70 g/2½ oz M&S Cashew Nuts
200 g/7 oz M&S Organic Polenta
M&S Sea Salt and Black Peppercorns, freshly ground

Cook's Tip
To make individual tatins instead of one large one, divide the mixture between four 350-ml/12-fl oz ovenproof dishes. Or, for smaller tatins to serve as an accompaniment, use six 250-ml/9-fl oz dishes. Bake for 15–20 minutes.

STICKY SPICED DUCK BREASTS WITH APPLE

Duck breasts are very easy to cook and have a richness that can take on spices and strong flavours really well. Duck's reputation as a fatty meat is much exaggerated, as a lot of fat drains off during cooking and the sweet-sharp, sticky juices coat the rich meat perfectly.

1. Slash the skin of the duck in a diamond pattern using a sharp knife. Place in a bowl with the sugar, vinegar and star anise, turning to coat evenly. Cover and leave to marinate in the refrigerator for 30 minutes or overnight.

2. Heat a heavy-based frying pan until very hot. Drain the duck, reserving the marinade, and place in the pan skin side down. When the fat sizzles, reduce the heat to medium and cook for 4–5 minutes, until golden brown. Turn over and cook for a further 4–5 minutes, until evenly golden brown but pink inside.

3. Transfer the duck breasts to a warmed plate, cover with foil and leave to stand for 10 minutes.

4. Core and thickly slice the apples. Tip the excess fat from the pan, then melt the butter. Stir in the apples and cook, stirring, for 1 minute or until golden. Add the reserved marinade, reduce the heat and simmer for 1 minute. Remove from the heat and discard the star anise.

5. Slice the duck, catching the juices, and arrange on serving plates. Stir the juices into the apples, then spoon over the duck to serve.

6. Serve with egg noodles, sprinkled with toasted sesame seeds and a drizzle of sesame oil.

Serves 4

4 medium duck breasts
4 tbsp M&S Dark Muscovado Sugar
4 tbsp M&S Cider Vinegar
4 pieces M&S Star Anise
2 dessert apples, such as Braeburn
25 g/1 oz butter
sesame oil, for drizzling
cooked M&S Fine Egg Noodles and toasted sesame seeds, to serve

Cook's Tip
For a stronger star anise flavour, remove the shiny seeds from the star-shaped pieces, crush them with a pestle and mortar to a powder and sprinkle into the sauce.

LEMON & PINK PEPPERCORN SEA BASS

This simple, elegant fish dish makes a trouble-free main course for a summer dinner party, and needs only a fresh mixed salad to complement it. Sea bass is a delicate fish that's good for baking or pan-frying.

1. Preheat the oven to 220°C/425°F/Gas Mark 7.

2. Lightly butter a wide, shallow, ovenproof dish and scatter the sliced onion over the base. Arrange the fish fillets on top in one layer, skin side down.

3. Coarsely grind the lemon and pink peppercorn mix and a little sea salt evenly over the fish fillets, then dot the remaining butter over the top. Pour the white wine around the fish.

4. Bake in the preheated oven for 20–25 minutes (depending on the thickness of the fish), or until the fish flakes easily when tested with a fork.

5. Meanwhile, cook the rice in lightly salted boiling water, according to the pack directions, for about 18 minutes, until just tender. Drain well, season lightly with lemon and pink peppercorn mix, and fluff up with a fork.

6. Spoon the rice onto 4 serving plates and arrange 2 fish fillets on each, overlapping. Spoon over the juices and onions and serve with lemon wedges.

Serves 4

25 g/1 oz butter
1 small red onion, very thinly sliced
8 sea bass fillets, about 600 g/1 lb 5 oz total weight
M&S Lemon & Pink Peppercorn Mill
M&S Sea Salt
100 ml/4 fl oz dry white wine
300 g/10½ oz M&S Long Grain & Wild Rice and lemon wedges, to serve

Cook's Tip

To use the rest of the M&S Lemon & Pink Peppercorn Mill, try adding a generous grinding to fluffy mashed potato or sweet potato. Grind it into a simple oil and vinegar salad dressing, to taste, or make a quick dip with cream cheese, chopped chives and a grinding of lemon and pink peppercorn mix.

Puddings & Desserts

ROSE PANNA COTTA CREAMS WITH RASPBERRY COMPÔTE

Lighter than a classic Italian panna cotta, this lower-fat version is delicately scented with rose water, and partnered with a tangy raspberry compôte for a stunning dinner party dessert. The fruit can be varied, depending on the season — try other berries, or tropical fruits such as mango or lychees.

1. Soak the gelatine leaves in 100 ml/3½ fl oz of the milk for 10 minutes, until soft.

2. Meanwhile, place the remaining milk, the cream and the sugar in a saucepan and heat gently until almost boiling. Pour onto the gelatine, stirring until the leaves have completely dissolved. Stir in the rose water.

3. Pour the mixture into four 175 ml/6 fl oz ramekins or metal pudding moulds. Chill in the refrigerator until set – at least 2 hours.

4. Meanwhile, make the raspberry compôte. Place the caster sugar and raspberry vinegar in a small saucepan, stir over a medium heat until the sugar dissolves, then boil for about 1 minute to reduce slightly to a light syrup. Place the raspberries in a bowl, pour over the syrup and stir lightly. Leave to stand until the panna cotta is set.

5. To serve, run a small knife around the edge of each panna cotta and dip the base of the mould quickly into hot water to loosen, then turn out onto serving plates. Add a spoonful of raspberry compôte and decorate with mint leaves.

Serves 4

4 leaves M&S Fine Leaf Gelatine
450 ml/16 fl oz semi-skimmed milk
150 ml/5 fl oz single cream
75 g/2½ oz M&S Organic Caster Sugar
½ tsp M&S Rose Water
fresh mint leaves or fresh pink rose petals, to decorate

Raspberry Compôte

75 g/2¾ oz M&S Organic Caster Sugar
3 tbsp M&S Raspberry Vinegar
200 g/7 oz fresh or frozen raspberries

Cook's Tip
If you don't have ramekin dishes or individual pudding moulds, four straight-sided teacups or short tumblers make a good alternative.

STICKY BANANA & COCONUT SPONGE PUDDINGS

You may think that 'proper' puddings take ages to make, but this easy, all-in-one pud is mixed within minutes. And, because it's baked in individual dishes, it's cooked in less than half an hour. This is a useful recipe for anyone on a dairy-free diet, as it uses oil for the mix.

1. Preheat the oven to 180°C/350°F/Gas Mark 4. Brush four 150 ml/5 fl oz metal pudding basins with a little of the oil. Spoon a tablespoon of golden syrup into each basin.

2. Place the banana, sugar, egg, flour and desiccated coconut in a food processor bowl and process for about 30 seconds to mix to a smooth batter.

3. Divide the mixture between the basins. Place on a baking sheet in the preheated oven and bake for 25–30 minutes, until well-risen, golden and firm to the touch.

4. Run a small knife around the edge of each pudding and turn out onto serving plates. Scatter the coconut flakes over and serve with yogurt.

Serves 4
75 ml/2½ fl oz M&S Pure Sunflower Oil
4 tbsp M&S Golden Syrup
1 large ripe banana
70 g/2½ oz M&S Organic Caster Sugar
1 egg
100 g/3½ oz M&S Organic Self Raising Flour
25 g/1 oz M&S Desiccated Coconut
15 g/½ oz M&S Coconut Flakes, lightly toasted
natural yogurt or low-fat custard, to serve

Cook's Tip
For a change of topping, the golden syrup could be replaced with a spoonful of your favourite jam or with clear honey. If you don't have individual pudding basins, use ramekins or any small ovenproof dishes to bake the puddings.

ALMOND & CARDAMOM RICE PUDDING BRÛLÉES

A modern twist on an old favourite — these little cardamom-scented rice puddings are finished with a topping of crunchy whole almonds under a caramelized glaze. If you're entertaining, the basic puds can be made several hours in advance, ready to brûlée when you're ready.

1. Place the rice, milk, sugar, cardamom pods and butter in a saucepan and bring almost to the boil. Reduce the heat to low, then cover and simmer gently for 30–35 minutes, until the rice is tender and most of the liquid is absorbed.

2. Preheat a grill to very hot. Spoon the rice mixture into four 150 ml/5 fl oz flameproof dishes set on a baking sheet. Arrange the almonds on top, pressing them slightly into the rice. Sprinkle the top of each dish with 1 tablespoon of sugar. Grill for 2–3 minutes, until the sugar melts and caramelizes. Alternatively, use a kitchen blowtorch.

3. Remove and cool for 10 minutes to serve warm, or cool completely, then chill before serving.

Serves 4
75 g/2¾ oz M&S Pudding Rice
600 ml/1 pint semi-skimmed milk
25 g/1 oz M&S Organic Caster
  sugar, plus 4 tbsp for sprinkling
2 M&S Cardamom Pods, lightly
  crushed and husks removed
15 g/½ oz unsalted butter
35 g/1¼ oz M&S Whole
  Almonds, blanched and
  skinned

Cook's Tip
To blanch the almonds quickly and easily, pour over boiling water to cover and leave for 1 minute, then drain and rinse in cold water; the skins should just slip off. If you prefer, the whole almonds can be replaced with M&S Flaked Almonds.

MOCHA HAZELNUT MESS

Lavish and lovely, this indulgent sweet treat is a good standby for a special dessert when you're short of time. A pack of ready-made mini meringues, either chocolate or plain, is a useful storecupboard item for whipping up a quick dessert, as they combine particularly well with fruits, nuts or creamy mixtures.

1. Preheat the grill to hot. Spread out the hazelnuts on a baking sheet and toast under the grill until lightly browned, shaking occasionally to toast evenly. Cool slightly, then rub lightly to remove any loose skins.

2. Roughly chop the hazelnuts. Crumble the meringues lightly with your fingers. Stir the coffee extract evenly into the yogurt, then lightly stir in the meringues with half the hazelnuts.

3. Spoon the mixture into 4 stemmed glasses and chill, for up to an hour, until required. Stir the remaining hazelnuts into the maple syrup, and spoon over the desserts just before serving.

Serves 4
100-g/3½-oz pack M&S Organic Hazelnuts
1 pack 20 M&S Belgian Chocolate Mini Meringues
1 tsp M&S Coffee Extract
400 g/14 oz Greek-style yogurt
2 tbsp maple syrup or clear honey, to serve

Cook's Tip
For a lighter, lower-fat version of the recipe, the Greek yogurt can be replaced with the same quantity of low-fat plain yogurt. Or, for an extra lavish, really grown-up dessert, replace the Greek yogurt with crème fraîche and add a splash of brandy or rum with the coffee essence.

MULLED PEARS IN RED WINE

Warmly spiced and richly coloured, this festive winter recipe is perfect for Christmas entertaining. Don't worry about the alcohol, as most of it is evaporated off during cooking. Cranberries not only add colour to the dish but give it a slightly tangy flavour, a perfect contrast to balance the sweet pears.

1. Pour the wine into a wide, heavy-based saucepan and stir in the sugar, bay leaves and cloves. Heat gently, stirring to dissolve the sugar. Remove from the heat and stir in the cranberries.

2. Peel and halve the pears, then scoop out the core from each half with a teaspoon. Add to the wine in the pan, in a single layer.

3. Return the pan to the heat and bring to the boil, then reduce to a gentle simmer. Cover and cook over a low heat for 35–40 minutes, gently turning the pears once, until tender. The cooking time will depend on the ripeness of the pears.

4. Lift out the pears and cranberries with a draining spoon and place in a serving dish. Place the pan back on a high heat and boil for about 5 minutes to reduce to about 200 ml/7 fl oz. Strain over the pears and sprinkle with toasted pecan nuts or walnuts.

5. Serve warm or cold, with a spoonful of whipped cream.

Serves 4

1 bottle red wine, such as claret
60 g/2¼ oz M&S Fairtrade Golden Granulated Sugar
2 M&S Dried Bay Leaves
3 M&S Whole Cloves
85 g/3 oz M&S Dried Cranberries
4 ripe but firm pears, such as Conference
70 g/2½ oz toasted pecan nuts or walnuts
whipped cream or crème fraîche, to serve

Cook's Tip

For a lighter flavour, the pears can be poached in cranberry juice, or cranberry and raspberry juice, instead of the red wine. Cook as in the recipe, adjusting the amount of sugar to taste. The colour will be paler than for pears cooked in wine.

PAN-ROASTED NECTARINE TARTLETS

A really stunning dessert made in minutes and you only have to cheat slightly, by using ready-made pastry cases. Nectarines are a good choice for the filling and the ginger and lime really bring out their flavour, but you can also use plums, dessert apples or bananas for a winter dessert.

1. Lay out the pastry tartlets on a board and spoon the yogurt into them, dividing evenly.

2. Halve and stone the nectarines and slice each fruit into about 8 slices. Melt the butter in a wide, heavy-based frying pan and stir in the sugar and ginger, stirring on a moderate heat until bubbling.

3. Add the sliced fruit and stir over a high heat for 1–2 minutes, until beginning to caramelize. Quickly stir in the lime juice, then remove from the heat. Lift out the nectarines with a draining spoon and spoon onto the tartlets.

4. Spoon the caramelized juices over the fruit and serve immediately. If the juices are too thick, add a tablespoon of water and stir until smooth.

Serves 8

1 pack of 8 M&S All Butter
   Pastry Tartlets
300 g/10½ oz Greek-style yogurt
4 small ripe nectarines
55 g/2 oz unsalted butter
55 g/2 oz M&S Fairtrade
   Demerara Sugar
1 tsp M&S Ground Ginger
3 tbsp M&S Organic Lime Juice

Cook's Tip
The pan-roasted, caramelized nectarines with their syrupy juices are delicious spooned over vanilla ice cream and sprinkled with chopped nuts. Or, for a cool summer dessert, why not pop a scoop of ice cream into each sweet pastry tartlet and top with the fruit as in the recipe — irresistible!

BRIOCHE BREAD & BUTTER PUDDING

The ultimate in bread and butter puddings, and you'll be surprised how speedy it is to make. Brioche is already quite buttery so there's no need to spread each slice with butter. Just layer with fruit and nuts, then sprinkle with ready-made cinnamon sugar for the correct balance of spice and sweetness.

1. Preheat the oven to 180°C/350°F/Gas Mark 4. Brush a 1.4-litre/2½-pint ovenproof dish with a little of the butter.

2. Cut the brioche slices in half diagonally to make triangles, then arrange overlapping in the dish, sprinkling with the dried fruit and nuts as you go.

3. Sprinkle with the rum if using and half the cinnamon sugar. Beat together the eggs and milk, then pour evenly over the brioche and fruit. Drizzle over the remaining butter and sprinkle with the remaining cinnamon sugar.

4. Bake in the preheated oven for 35–40 minutes, or until just set and golden brown. Serve warm, as it is, or with pouring cream.

Serves 4

15 g/½ oz butter, melted
6 slices from a brioche loaf (about 175 g/6 oz total)
85 g/3 oz M&S Organic Mixed Fruit
55 g/2 oz M&S Organic Chopped Mixed Nuts
2 tbsp dark rum (optional)
2 tbsp M&S Cinnamon Sugar
2 eggs
600 ml/1 pint milk

Cook's Tip
For a chocolate bread and butter pudding, omit the fruit and nuts from the recipe and replace with a 200-g/7-oz pack of M&S Plain Chocolate Drops. Finish and bake as in the recipe.

RHUBARB & ORANGE CRUMBLE TART

A refreshing change from an old-fashioned fruit crumble, this easy tart is very quick to make, as even the fresh fruit needs very little preparation. If rhubarb is not in season, use sliced Bramley apples or gooseberries instead for a tangy-sweet filling.

1. Preheat the oven to 200°C/400°F/Gas Mark 6. Place the pastry case on a baking sheet.

2. Finely grate the zest from the orange and reserve. With a sharp knife, cut away all the remaining peel and white pith. Remove the segments, catching all the juices in a bowl.

3. Place the orange juice, rhubarb and sugar in a wide saucepan and cook over a medium heat, stirring occasionally, for 4–6 minutes or until almost tender. Remove from the heat, strain off as much juice as possible and reserve the juice. Add the orange segments to the rhubarb and spoon into the pastry case.

4. Rub the butter into the crumble mix until it resembles breadcrumbs. Stir in the ground almonds. Spread half the mixture (see Cook's Tip) over the fruit in the pastry case, without pressing down.

5. Bake the crumble tart in the preheated oven for about 20 minutes or until golden brown. Serve warm, scattered with shreds of orange zest, with the reserved juices drizzled over.

Serves 4
1 M&S All Butter Pastry Case
1 large orange
500 g/1 lb 2 oz pink rhubarb, sliced
60 g/2¼ oz M&S Organic Caster Sugar
100 g/3½ oz cold unsalted butter
360-g/12½-oz pack M&S Crumble Mix (see Cook's Tip)
55 g/2 oz M&S Organic Ground Almonds

Cook's Tip
The quantity of topping is enough for two tarts, so if you don't wish to use it all at once, store in the refrigerator for up to a week, or freeze for up to 2 months. It's ready to sprinkle over another crumble tart, or to top stewed fruit or canned pie filling for a quick crumble pudding.

DARK CHOCOLATE VANILLA PUFFS

Yes, they're soufflés, but no need to panic — they're the simplest, most chocolatey soufflés ever. Chocolate and vanilla is a heavenly combination, and the extra kick of chocolate and brandy sauce added at the end makes these a really special dinner party dessert.

1. Preheat the oven to 200°C/400°F/Gas Mark 6 and place a baking sheet on a middle shelf. Lightly butter four 150-ml/ 5-fl oz ramekins.

2. Place 140 g/5 oz of the chocolate drops in a small bowl over a saucepan of hot water and leave until just melted.

3. Beat together the egg yolks, icing sugar, vanilla seeds and cornflour in a bowl until smooth. Remove the chocolate from the heat and quickly stir into the egg yolk mixture.

4. Whisk the egg whites in a clean bowl until they are stiff enough to hold their shape. Stir a spoonful of egg white into the chocolate mixture, then fold in the rest lightly and evenly with a metal spoon.

5. Divide the mixture between the ramekins, place them on the baking sheet and sprinkle the tops with chocolate vermicelli. Bake in the preheated oven for 15–20 minutes, until well risen and almost firm to the touch.

6. Meanwhile, melt the remaining chocolate drops with the brandy in a bowl over hot water. Remove the puffs from the oven and quickly make a hole in the top of each with a teaspoon. Drizzle in the brandy sauce and serve immediately.

Serves 4
1 tbsp melted unsalted butter
200 g/7 oz M&S Plain Chocolate Drops
3 eggs, separated
55 g/2 oz M&S Organic Icing Sugar
seeds from 1 M&S Vanilla Pod
1 tsp cornflour
1 tbsp M&S Chocolate Vermicelli
1 tbsp brandy

Cook's Tip
For a creamier sauce to serve with the puddings, melt the chocolate and brandy with 4 tablespoons of crème fraîche, stirring until smooth. Drizzle over the puddings before serving.

Baking

CHERRY CUP CAKES

Pretty little cup cakes are perfect for parties of all kinds, and for all ages. They're quick to mix and bake, and children will love to help make and decorate them. For a healthier topping, use slices of apple brushed with lemon juice.

1. Preheat the oven to 190°C/375°F/Gas Mark 5. Place 18 paper cup cake cases in bun tins, or arrange on a baking sheet.

2. Sift the flour and baking powder into a bowl and add the margarine, sugar, eggs, and vanilla extract. Beat thoroughly with a wooden spoon until just smooth. Stir in the cherries.

3. Spoon the mixture into the paper cases and bake in the preheated oven for 15–20 minutes, until golden brown and firm to the touch. Lift onto a wire rack to cool.

4. To decorate, roll out the soft icing fairly thinly and cut eighteen rounds with a 5.5-cm/2¼-inch fluted biscuit cutter. Place the rounds on top of the cakes, brush with boiled water and then scatter the sprinkles over before the icing sets.

Makes 18
150 g/5½ oz M&S Organic Self Raising Flour
1 tsp M&S Baking Powder
125 g/4½ oz soft margarine (not low-fat spread)
125 g/4½ oz M&S Organic Caster Sugar
2 eggs
½ tsp M&S Organic Vanilla Extract
100 g/3½ oz M&S Glacé Cherries, chopped

To decorate
500-g/1 lb 2-oz pack M&S Ready to roll Soft Icing
1 tbsp M&S Sprinkles

You will need
18 M&S Cup Cake Cases

Cook's Tip
For adult celebrations, finish the cup cakes with a round of soft icing and a quick brush of brandy topped with sprinkles, or crystallized rose petals for a more sophisticated look For children, use M&S Writing Icing to add names or initials to the cakes.

MEDITERRANEAN BREAD SPIRALS

Making your own bread is really satisfying, especially when you can create something as interesting as these little bread rolls. They're packed with Mediterranean flavours, and are great to pack for summer picnics or outdoor lunches. You could also try them warm with a bowl of soup for a quick, satisfying meal.

1. Place the flour in a bowl and stir in the salt and yeast. Make a well in the centre and stir in the water and oil. Bring the dough together with your hands, then turn out onto a lightly floured surface and knead for 5–10 minutes until smooth.

2. Return the dough to the bowl, cover with a clean, damp tea towel and leave to rest for 10 minutes. Turn out and roll out to a large rectangle about 35 x 45 cm/14 x 18 inches.

3. Spread the pesto over the dough, then scatter with sundried tomatoes, torn strips of Parma ham and shavings of Parmesan cheese. Roll up the dough from one long side to enclose the filling, like a long Swiss roll.

4. Sprinkle a large baking sheet with polenta. Using a sharp knife, cut the dough into about 10 diagonal slices and place on the baking sheet. Cover with a clean, damp tea towel and leave in a warm place for 45 minutes–1 hour, until doubled in size.

5. Meanwhile, preheat the oven to 220°C/425°F/Gas Mark 7. Bake the bread spirals in the preheated oven for 20–25 minutes, until well-risen and golden brown. Cool on a wire rack.

Makes 10

500 g/1 lb 2 oz M&S Organic Bread Flour, plus extra for dusting
2 tsp M&S Sea Salt
6 g/4 oz sachet easy-blend dried yeast
350 ml/12 fl oz lukewarm water
2 tbsp olive oil
4 tbsp pesto
65-g/2¼-oz pack M&S Italian Sundried Tomatoes, soaked, drained and chopped
8 thin slices Parma ham or prosciutto
25 g/1 oz Parmesan cheese shavings
M&S Organic Polenta, for sprinkling

Cook's Tip
If time is short, use a pack of M&S Bread Mix for a quicker result. Try these alternative fillings: Spread with passata, sprinkle with roasted garlic, flaked chillies and pine nuts. Brush with olive oil, sprinkle with crumbled blue cheese and rosemary. Spread with red pesto, sprinkle with chopped black olives and crumbled feta cheese.

CHOCOLATE & ORANGE SEMOLINA CAKE

This unusual chocolate cake is made without flour, using semolina instead to give a lovely crumbly texture, with juicy chunks of orange for a fresh flavour. Serve it plain, or dressed up with shreds of orange zest for a more special occasion.

1. Preheat the oven to 180°C/350°F/Gas Mark 4. Grease and base-line a 20-cm/8-inch cake tin.

2. Finely grate the zest from the orange and reserve. With a sharp knife, cut away all the remaining peel and white pith, then cut the flesh into small pieces, catching the juices.

3. Place the sugar and eggs in a bowl and whisk hard with an electric whisk until pale and foamy. Whisk in the butter gradually, pouring a thin steady stream as you whisk. Sift over the semolina, cocoa powder and baking powder, and fold in lightly and evenly. Stir in the orange pieces and their juice to mix to a soft batter.

4. Spread the mixture in the tin, smoothing level with a palette knife. Bake in the preheated oven for 35–40 minutes, until just firm to the touch. Leave to cool in the tin for 5 minutes, then turn out onto a wire rack to cool.

5. To decorate, scatter with the reserved shreds of orange zest and sprinkle with icing sugar.

Serves 8

85 g/3 oz unsalted butter, melted, plus extra for greasing
1 large orange
100 g/3½ oz M&S Organic Caster Sugar
2 eggs
175 g/6 oz M&S Semolina
55 g/2 oz M&S Organic Fairtrade Cocoa Powder
1½ tsp M&S Baking Powder
M&S Organic Icing Sugar, to decorate

Cook's Tip

The amount of juice in oranges varies, so if the mixture seems too dry, stir in an additional 1-2 tablespoons of orange juice to soften it. For a really lavish touch of flavour drizzle 1-2 tablespoons of orange liqueur, such as Cointreau or Grand Marnier, over the cake when it comes out of the oven.

STRAWBERRY VANILLA CHEESECAKE GÂTEAU

There's no better way to indulge a friend or loved one than by baking them a cake, so this special gâteau will come in useful for those birthdays and party occasions when something lavish is called for. Don't worry, it won't take much of your time — not if you cheat and use a sponge cake mix!

1. Preheat the oven to 190°C/375°F/Gas Mark 5. Grease and line two 18-cm/7-inch sandwich cake tins.

2. Make up the cake mix according to the pack directions, using the butter, eggs and milk. Divide between the tins and bake in the preheated oven for 25–30 minutes.

3. Remove from the oven, leave to cool in the tins for a few minutes, then turn out onto a wire rack to finish cooling completely.

4. Add the icing sachet from the cake mix pack to the mascarpone and beat until smooth. Reserve 4–6 strawberries for decoration and chop the rest. Stir the chopped strawberries and vanilla extract into the mascarpone cheese.

5. Spoon the strawberry mixture onto one of the cakes, piling it up slightly in the centre. Drizzle the sachet of jam from the cake mix pack over the filling. Position the second cake on top of the filling and cut into 6 slices.

6. Decorate with the reserved strawberries and add a generous sprinkling of icing sugar to serve.

Serves 6
60 g/2¼ oz butter or margarine
1 pack M&S Victoria Sponge
  Cake Mix
2 eggs
150 ml/5 fl oz milk
70 g/2½ oz mascarpone cheese
200 g/7 oz strawberries
½ tsp M&S Organic Vanilla
  Extract
M&S Organic Icing Sugar,
  for sprinkling

Cook's Tip
If what you need is a gâteau entirely from the storecupboard, just make up the cake and filling according to the normal pack directions, and replace the strawberries with canned fruit such as pineapple or peaches.

DATE & NUT CRUMBLE BARS

These crumbly date and nut bars have a light, lemony flavour. Gluten free cakes and bakes are often hard to find, but this one fits the bill as it's made with gluten free flour and oats, cutting out any wheat allergy worries for coeliacs or anyone with wheat intolerance.

1. Preheat the oven to 190°C/375°F/Gas Mark 5. Lightly grease a 31 x 17-cm/12½ x 6½-inch rectangular cake tin.

2. Place the butter in a mixing bowl with the flour and oats, and rub the butter into the dry ingredients with your fingers to make coarse crumbs (you can do this in a food processor). Stir in 150 g/5½ oz of the sugar, the lemon rind and half the chopped nuts, mixing to a crumbly dough.

3. Tip about two thirds of the mix into the tin and press with your knuckles to spread evenly over the base. Mix the remaining dough with the reserved nuts, stirring to make a crumbly mixture.

4. Place the dates in a small saucepan with the remaining sugar, the lemon juice and the mixed spice. Stir until boiling, then simmer for 1–2 minutes until most of the juices are absorbed. Spread over the dough in the tin, then top with the crumble mixture, pressing down lightly.

5. Bake in the preheated oven for 35–40 minutes, until golden brown. Remove from the oven and cool for about 30 minutes, then cut into the number of bars required and leave to cool completely in the tin.

Makes about 12

250 g/9 oz unsalted butter, plus extra for greasing
225 g/8 oz M&S Gluten Free Plain Flour
200 g/7 oz porridge oats
175 g/6 oz M&S Light Muscovado Sugar
finely grated rind and juice of 1 lemon
100-g/3½-oz pack M&S Organic Chopped Mixed Nuts
250-g/9-oz pack M&S Organic Deglet Noor Dates, chopped
½ tsp M&S Mixed Spice

Cook's Tip
Once cooled, the bars can be stored for 3-4 days in a covered container. You could also pack them into a freezer container, seal and freeze for up to 2 months. Thaw at room temperature. If you don't have a rectangular tin, use one with a similar capacity, such as a 23-cm/9-inch square tin.

APRICOT ALMOND CROISSANTS

Irresistibly sweet and delicately almond-scented, these little croissant-shaped pastries make a lovely coffee-time or after-dinner treat, or can be served alongside a light dessert, such as a fruit sorbet. Warm them for a few minutes in a hot oven before serving to enjoy them at their best.

Makes 8

butter, for greasing
425-g/15-oz pack puff pastry, thawed
115 g/4 oz M&S Dried Organic Apricots, roughly chopped
175 g/6 oz M&S Ready to roll Natural Marzipan
1 tbsp milk, for glazing
2 tbsp M&S Apricot Glaze
25 g/1 oz M&S Organic Flaked Almonds, toasted

1. Preheat the oven to 220°C/425°F/Gas Mark 7. Lightly grease a large baking sheet.

2. Lay out the 2 pastry sheets and trim each to a square. Cut each square into 4 triangles, about 21 x 15 x 15 cm/ 8¼ x 6 x 6 inches. Divide the apricots between the triangles, placing them in the centre. Roll the marzipan into 8 small sausage shapes and place on top of the apricots.

3. Roll up each triangle from the longest side to enclose the apricots and marzipan. Place them on the baking sheet, turning the outer points in towards each other to resemble croissants. Brush lightly with milk, then bake in the preheated oven for 15–20 minutes, until golden brown and crisp.

4. Remove the pastries from the oven and squeeze a dab of apricot glaze on each, brushing it over the pastry while still warm. Sprinkle with toasted flaked almonds and place on a wire rack to cool.

Cook's Tip
To use up the rest of the packs of marzipan and apricots, cut a slit down one side of each apricot to make a pocket. Tuck walnut-sized balls of marzipan into each apricot, pressing together lightly. Place in M&S Mini Cake Cases. Serve as petit fours, or pack into a pretty box for a gift.

CHUNKY APPLE & CHEESE MUFFINS

These savoury fruit and cheese muffins are really useful for a quick breakfast on the run, or to brighten up an everyday lunchbox. Serve fresh to enjoy them at their best, or pop them in the microwave for a few seconds to warm slightly.

1. Preheat the oven to 190°C/375°F/Gas Mark 5. Arrange the muffin cases in a muffin tray or on a baking sheet.

2. Sift the flour, baking powder and salt into a large bowl and make a well in the centre. Add the oil, yogurt, eggs and milk, then mix well to combine evenly.

3. Reserve about 2 tablespoons of the cheese and add the rest to the bowl with the apples and sultanas, stirring lightly to mix.

4. Spoon the mixture into the muffin cases and sprinkle with the reserved cheese. Bake in the preheated oven for 20–25 minutes, or until well risen and golden brown. Leave to cool on a wire rack.

Makes 12
250 g/9 oz M&S Organic Plain Flour
1 tbsp M&S Baking Powder
½ tsp M&S Sea Salt
4 tbsp M&S Pure Sunflower Oil
150 g/5 oz natural low-fat yogurt
2 eggs, beaten
125 ml/4 fl oz milk
140 g/5 oz extra mature Cheddar cheese, coarsely grated
2 dessert apples, such as Cox or Gala, cored and cut into 5-mm/¼-inch dice
55 g/2 oz M&S Organic Sultanas

You will need
12 M&S Muffin Cases

Cook's Tip
Cheese, apple and walnut muffins: a muffin with a nuttier, spicier flavour. Replace the sultanas with chopped walnuts or mixed chopped nuts and add 1 tbsp wholegrain mustard to the mix with the cheese. Bake the muffins as in the main recipe.

GINGERBREAD SQUARES WITH LEMON DRIZZLE

Made with an all-in-one method that doesn't even need an electric mixer, this warmly spiced ginger cake is a good family favourite. It keeps well, so make sure you hide some away for later or it will all disappear in minutes!

1. Preheat the oven to 180°C/350°F/Gas Mark 4. Grease a 19-cm/7½-inch square cake tin and base-line with non-stick baking paper.

2. Sift the flour and ginger together into a bowl. In a separate bowl, beat together the eggs, sugar, treacle, milk and oil. Make a well in the flour and add the liquid mixture, beating thoroughly to make a smooth batter.

3. Pour the batter mixture into the tin and bake in the preheated oven for 25–30 minutes, or until risen and springy to the touch. Cool in the tin for 5 minutes, then turn out and finish cooling on a wire rack.

4. Mix the icing sugar with the lemon extract and enough water to make a fairly thick paste. Drizzle over the cake and sprinkle with silver balls. Cut into 9 squares when set.

Makes 9

butter, for greasing
175 g/6 oz M&S Organic Self Raising Flour
1 tbsp M&S Ground Ginger
2 eggs
100 g/3½ oz M&S Light Muscovado Sugar
4 tbsp M&S Black Treacle
4 tbsp milk
4 tbsp M&S Pure Sunflower Oil

To decorate
100 g/3½ oz M&S Organic Icing Sugar
½ tsp M&S Lemon Extract
1 tbsp M&S Silver Balls

Cook's Tip
The ginger cake improves with keeping and can be stored successfully for a week in a tin with a tightly-fitting lid, or wrapped in foil. Alternatively, pack in an airtight box or polythene bag and freeze for up to 2 months. Thaw at room temperature.

CRUNCHY SEED 'N' SPICE COOKIES

Warmly spiced and coated in crunchy sunflower seeds, these biscuits are very difficult to leave alone, so it's worth making a big batch. Sunflower seeds are a natural source of the antioxidant vitamin E.

1. Preheat the oven to 200°C/400°F/Gas Mark 6. Lightly butter two baking sheets.

2. Using an electric hand mixer, cream together the butter and sugar until soft and fluffy. Add the egg and beat thoroughly, then stir in the flour, caraway seeds and nutmeg, mixing evenly to a fairly stiff dough.

3. Roll heaped teaspoonfuls of dough into walnut-sized balls with your hands. Toss them roughly in the sunflower seeds to coat lightly, then arrange on the baking sheets and press lightly with your fingers to flatten slightly.

4. Bake the cookies in the preheated oven for 12–15 minutes, or until golden brown. Lift onto a wire rack to cool.

Makes about 22
85 g/3 oz unsalted butter, plus extra for greasing
85 g/3 oz M&S Light Muscovado Sugar
1 egg, beaten
225 g/8 oz M&S Organic Plain Flour
1 tsp M&S Caraway Seeds
1 tsp freshly grated M&S Whole Nutmeg
55 g/2 oz M&S Organic Sunflower Seeds

Cook's Tip
The cookies will freeze successfully for up to 3 months. Cool completely, then pack them in an airtight box or polythene bag, seal and freeze. Thaw at room temperature or, if time is tight, pop the cookies on a baking sheet and place in a moderate oven for 4–5 minutes.

easy
Pasta

easy
Chicken

Also available in
YOUR M&S are a wide range
of inspirational cookbooks
including the bestselling
Easy range

easy
Curries

Visit your local M&S for more details.
All titles listed are subject to availability.

easy
Healthy